THE PORT OF CHEPSTOW

by Ivor Waters

THE CHEPSTOW SOCIETY,
CHEPSTOW, GWENT.

ISBN : 0 900278 37 4

Number 30 in the Chepstow Society Pamphlet Series

PRINTED IN GREAT BRITAIN IN 1977 BY
F. G. COMBER
2 ST. MARY STREET
CHEPSTOW, GWENT, NP6 5EU

ACKNOWLEDGMENTS

I should like to thank everyone who has lent me books, documents, or illustrations, or helped me in any way, including S. F. Aitken, Dr. J. H. Andrews, W. H. Baker and Gwent County Record Office, Grahame Farr, Norman Mutton, Harry Paar, Mrs Jane Pearson and Chepstow Museum, B. J. Stevens (for the cover illustration), Dr. D. G. Tucker, Bryan Woodfield, the librarians and staffs of Newport Reference Library, Gwent County Library, Cardiff Reference Library and the Public Record Office, my wife, and the printer F. G. Comber and his staff.

The Port of Chepstow

IN THE BEGINNING

It is always fascinating to watch great ships entering or leaving harbour, although one modern dock may look very much like another. But perhaps the imagination is stirred even more strongly by the intimacy of a small river port which has not greatly altered since the days of sail. Chepstow seamen never discovered new lands, or transported slaves across the ocean, or "held the gorgeous east in fee," but no doubt they made many an adventurous voyage, since bare facts tell us of cargoes of wine from Bordeaux and Oporto, stockfish from Iceland, and timber from the Baltic and North America.

Chepstow custom house closed in 1882 and there was an end to foreign trade. Gradually warehouses and quays were neglected, but even to-day we can stand on the site of an 18th. century dry dock by the last of the warehouses which held corn, oak bark, and wine, and, as we walk along the former wharves which supplied the naval dockyards with timber, we can recall a maritime past which goes back to the time of the Lords of the Marches of Wales.

We find shipping at Chepstow first mentioned in 1086, in Domesday Book, which states that the Earl of Hereford, William FitzOsborn, received an annual levy of 40 shillings from ships going up the river to the forest. After William's death, his son Roger began to build a town near what was then called Striguil castle, but he lost his estates after an unsuccessful rebellion against the Conqueror. According to Domesday Book,

William de Eu, the Lord of Tidenham, received £9 a year from the "toll of Strigoielg," but the jury considered he had "no more by right than ten pounds from the toll of Strigoielg, even if it were worth a hundred pounds."

When Henry II became King in 1154 he gave almost a monopoly of the wine trade to the Bordeaux merchants of his queen's native Aquitaine. The vineyards were under English rule for three centuries, at a time when the powerful lords of Chepstow were enjoying the privileges granted by the Conqueror to the Lords of the Marches whereby they ruled with virtually no interference from the King. However, there is no evidence that Chepstow merchants were able to benefit from the privileges during the 12th. century.

In 1170, the lord of Chepstow, Richard de Clare (usually known as Strongbow) conquered Ireland with the encouragement of Henry II and gained vast estates there. The King began to fear that his subject was becoming too powerful and fitted out a fleet at Newnham near the lordship of Striguil in order to make a token conquest of Ireland himself. The fleet reached Waterford on October 18th, 1171, but the King travelled through Chepstow overland and sailed from Milford, returning the following year by the same route. Strongbow held his Irish estates until his death in 1176, so it is likely that a direct trade began between Chepstow and Ireland. Strongbow's Irish widow was Countess of Striguil, but the King held the castle, as guardian of the infant heiress Isabella, until her marriage to the powerful William Marshal.

The chief import into England continued to be wine, and this began to be taxed by a system called prisage, the right of the King to take from every English vessel importing 20 or more tuns of wine one tun from before the mast and one tun from behind the mast, where the better wine was placed to keep it safe from the sea. The payment of "ancient and just customs" is confirmed by the 41st. article of Magna Carta.

William Marshal attached great importance to the wine trade when he was Regent during the minority of Henry III, but apparently he considered himself exempt from prisage as a Marcher lord, and there were complaints that he did not allow the payment of customs to the King "en le port de Chipstouwe a graunt damage du roi."

In 1223 wine was taken up the Wye for the King's expedition into Wales and in 1258 Tintern stored wine on its way to Monmouth castle and made a warehouse charge of 2d. a day. The Abbot of Tintern's trade was chiefly in wool. He was a member of the staple at Bristol and had a ship of his own (William Powell, master) which was plundered by Robert Aiken of Bristol while on passage up the Wye in 1268.

EDWARD I AND ROGER BIGOD

In 1275 Edward I ended free trade by placing a custom on wool and on the less important export of hides. About 15 headports were set up, each with a Collector of Customs and a Controller to check the Collector. Other officials included Searchers (at first to prevent the export of precious metals and the import of false money, but later to prevent smuggling in general), Surveyors to check the Searchers, and Deputies in the smaller ports.

Chepstow was nominally controlled by Bristol, and a Chepstow ship with a cargo of hides is mentioned in Bristol customs accounts for April 12th 1292. The lord of Chepstow from 1270 to 1306 was Roger Bigod, Earl of Norfolk, who was mainly responsible for building Tintern Abbey, Chepstow castle, and the portwalls. He was Earl Marshal and a man of great power and arrogance, so it is unlikely that he allowed his "rights" to be diminished by his neighbours or by the King. There were complaints in 1282 about his "ports called Beachley, Strogoyle, and Tintern" where the Earl had "boats by which vension taken in the Forest is carried away." In 1286 he quarrelled with the dowager Countess of Gloucester after her tenants had thrown down palings of Chepstow Park. In 1291 the Earl of Gloucester's retainers raided the lands of

Roger Bigod, who had claimed the overlordship enjoyed by William Marshal, whereupon Roger destroyed the town of Trelleck. The King intervened and for a time there was peace on the frontier.

At the Parliament held in 1297, Edward I demanded that Roger Bigod should lead an expedition to Gascony while he took an army to Flanders. The Earl Marshal replied that it was his duty to go with the King, but not without him. It is reported that Edward shouted, "By God, Earl, you shall either go or hang" and that Roger replied, "By God, O King, I shall neither go nor hang."
He retired to Chepstow and on July 30th a writ was issued to the "Bailiffs of Chepstow" ordering them to equip certain ships which had returned from Gascony with salt, and to send them to Winchelsea for the King's expedition to Flanders. Presumably the writ was ignored. There was a reconciliation at the end of the year, and in 1298 Roger Bigod accompanied the King on his Scottish expedition, taking with him a hundred men.

In August, 1302 the Aquitaine merchants made an agreement with Edward I to pay butlerage on wine at 2s. a tun instead of prisage, and in the following year the *Carta Mercatoria* extended this duty to all aliens. The Chepstow merchants probably continued to pay prisage as before at a lower rate than Bristol traders paid to the Collector of Customs.

After his conquest of Wales in 1282, Edward I tried to curb the powers of the Lords of the Marches, but in the end the most he could extract from Roger Bigod was an agreement to surrender his lordship after his death in return for the promise of dower lands for his widow. Roger Bigod died on 11th December 1306 and the King seven months later, before he could carry out his intention of conferring Striguil on his infant son, Thomas de Brotherton.

ATTEMPTS TO RESTRICT THE MARCHER PRIVILEGES

Edward II appointed Hugh le Despenser as custodian of Striguil until 1310, when he was accused of neglecting the castle. Thomas de Brotherton became lord from 1310 and was made Earl Marshal in 1315, but the people of the town no doubt saw only his deputies and could not look upon a boy with the respect they had been forced to give to Roger Bigod. In May, 1311, Edward II ordered Chepstow to help him in the war against Scotland with one ship, supplied with men, armour, and victuals for seven weeks. "The Bailiffs, Good Men, and all the Community of the Town of Chepstow" replied that for the last seven years only four ships had belonged to the town, and of these three had been wrecked near Tenby and a fourth had gone to Gascony and had not returned. Moreover "they were in such poverty by the death of their liege lord Roger le Bygot, Earl Marshal" that they prayed the King to "have regard to their poverty until God mende their condition."

In 1312, John de Pateshulle, the deputy-constable, looted the castle and absconded. The history of the port is blank for a dozen years, except that on August 27th, 1323 Thomas de Brotherton leased Striguil for life to Hugh le Despenser, who had become the King's "favourite" and virtual ruler of the country.

In 1325 Edward II received reports on the number of ships available for an expedition to Gascony and was informed by Robert Bendyn, Admiral of the Fleet from the Mouth of the Thames Westwards, that at Chepstow Thomas Germeyn had one ship of 100 tons and another of 45 tons; John Cook had one ship of 80 tons; and William Chepeman had one ship of 60 tons.

In 1326 there are records of the smuggling of wool across the Wye for re-export and of attempts to make Chepstow ships pay tolls on the grounds that they had stopped in King's Road off the mouth of the Avon, showing that royal customs were still not being paid in the Wye. That same year the Queen became disgusted with the power the Despensers had over her husband and left for France, returning in September with an army to Harwich. Edward II, the Chancellor Robert de Baldock, and the Despensers fled west, reaching Chepstow on October 16th. Hugh le Despenser was sent to oppose the Queen at Bristol but was defeated and hanged. Chepstow castle surrendered without a siege and Edward II sailed on October 21st for Lundy and Ireland. Storms caused him to put in at Cardiff, he was captured, and on September 20th, 1327 murdered in Berkeley castle.

On October 8th John de la Pole and Henry Deorday were empowered to levy and collect 2s. on each cask of wine imported by foreign merchants into London and a dozen other places, including Chepstow. Roger Turtle and Hugh de Langbrugge were described as being collectors of the ancient custom of wool, hides, and woolfells, and of the "new customs" in "Bristoll et Cheppestowe." The first Chepstow ship we hear of by name was *La Mariote* (Philip Rikelyn, master), which on February 23rd, 1329/30 was carrying a cargo of hides. There followed more instances of attempts by customs officers to collect dues from ships carrying wine to Chepstow on the grounds that they had stopped in the King's Road, and in 1338 the new duties were resisted by seamen from both the ports mentioned. André Simon has related that on April 24th "a commission of oyer and terminer was issued touching the forcible taking away from Bristol, by men of Bristol and Chepstow, of a ship laden with wines, before the prises due to the king and the customs amounting to £40 had been paid." In this instance the men involved were apparently going beyond any claim to Marcher privileges, unless the vessel had been seized by customs officers on the northern side of the Severn.

Chepstow was specifically included in the headport of Bristol from September 1346, in time for the introduction of an order made on April 20th, the following year to collect custom on cloth "in every port of the realm." It was not thought worth while to employ customs officers in some of the poorer and more remote parts of the country such as Lancashire, Wales, and Cornwall.
Chepstow merchants probably continued as before when it suited them, because there are records of attempts being made in 1347 to prevent English merchants carrying wool and other goods across the Wye "out of the realm of England for the purpose of export, whereby the King was defrauded of his customs." It was understood that Chepstow was in fact a free port, but on the other hand Chepstow merchants, who probably included William Betesleye (Beachley) and John Shipman, traded in cloth from Bristol after the introduction of the order, so making the best of both worlds. In the reign of Richard II cloth was exported from Chepstow to Spain, and on November 5th, 1390 the *Marie* of Chepstow carried cloth from Bristol to Lisbon.

Seamen from Chepstow were almost certainly in the unsuccessful expedition of John of Gaunt, Duke of Lancaster, to Corunna to claim the throne of Spain, for in March, 1386, William Whitebread, John Polyn, and John Haly of Bristol were appointed to "provide ships and raise mariners in the ports of Bristoll, Bruggewater, Chepstowe and Axinter" as part of the fleet of 200 vessels. In February the following year William Clifford and William Merford of Coventry were licensed to buy 800 quarters of wheat in Worcestershire and Gloucestershire to export from Bristol, Newport and Chepstow in a Spanish ship "for the refreshment of our dearest uncle John, King of Castile, and of the legion of the Duke of Lancaster and others of our subjects." In the same year 1387, the mayor of Bristol was ordered to investigate English smugglers entering the Severn and running goods into Chepstow and Monmouth.

Importers often brought wine to Chepstow to unload into smaller boats for carriage across the Severn to Bristol and other places without paying the full tunnage dues. As a result, the Bristol customs officers were ordered in 1392 to enter the "creek" of Chepstow to levy duties at the national rate. They must have tried to carry out this order, because in 1395 a petition was sent to Parliament "on behalf of the merchants of the Welsh Marches" complaining of the Bristol customs activities. Possibly the officers became more cautious, for that same year attempts were made to levy tolls on the grounds that the Chepstow vessels had stopped in the King's Road or Bristol river.

ICELAND

In the early years of the 15th century English ships began to trade with Iceland. Fishing doggers from the east coast brought back wet fish, but Bristol and Chepstow vessels took iron, timber, wheat, wine, butter, honey, malt, and cloth to barter for stockfish caught and dried by the Icelanders. The King of Norway owned Iceland, but Norway itself was under Danish rule, and all fish caught off the coast of Iceland had to be taken to the staple at Bergen, controlled by the Hanseatic League. The Hanse had a "factory" in London with a monopoly of North European trade so, since the English could not take part in this, sailors defied the law and went direct to Iceland by the outer route and western Ireland.

Bristol was the chief port involved in this illegal trade, but Chepstow also sent ships, using the lodestone described in the *Libelle of Englyshe Policye* in 1436:

> Of Yseland to wryte is lytill nede
> Save of stokfische, yit for sothe in dede
> Out of Bristow and costis many one
> Men have practised by nedle and by stone
> Thiderwardes wythine a lytel whylle,
> Wythine XIJ yeres, and wythoute parille,
> Gone and comen.

The Icelanders were neglected by the Norwegians, so welcomed the opportunity to get exotic and manufactured goods from England in exchange for their fish, even though many of the smugglers were outlaws and murderers. Rowdy seamen quarrelled with the Danish officials and plundered and stole cattle, additional reasons for their being warned to keep away from Iceland. The Hanse complained to Henry V and he forbade the trade. More than 30 fishing vessels visited Iceland in 1413 and the merchants soon followed. In a storm in 1419, 25 English vessels were driven on the coast of Iceland in three hours.

Henry VI in 1430 prohibited the English by statute from going to Iceland but, as Power and Postan have pointed out, "The official records of the years following 1430 are strewn with the relics of ships and their cargoes forfeited to the King." Frequently offenders took their stockfish to Chepstow to avoid confiscation.

Then on April 28th, 1434, with much official flourish and reference to the friendship of Henry VI King of England and France and the Dominion of Ireland, with his dearest uncle the King of Norway and Sweden, a warrant was issued to the bailiffs and community of Chepstow to trade direct with Iceland

and Finmark for the purpose of obtaining fish or any other merchandise whatsoever. In 1436 so many vessels sailed to Iceland that half of them were unable to get a return cargo.

The trade declined about the middle of the century, but at least two ships went to Iceland from Bristol in 1480, so possibly an occasional vessel from Chepstow was also venturing to the "costes colde."

WINE TRADE

André Simon has recorded a ship called the "*Trynytat* of Chepyscolle" taking wine in 1444 to Hull, which like Chepstow and Cornwall, paid duties only to the local lord. Wine ships from Chepstow occur in the accounts of the Constable of Bordeaux at about this time and even after the expulsion of the English in 1453. Bristol was, after London, the biggest importer of wine, yet in one month in May, 1461 the Chepstow ships *Christopher, Margaret, Marie* and *Julian* took seven cargoes to Bristol from the Wye totalling 4,977 gallons. John Walter was granted a licence to ship "undrinkable" wine to Ireland from Bristol in *Le Cristofre*.

Not much can be gleaned about shipping during the following half-century except from occasional records of litigation, but it appears that Chepstow merchants William Taillour and Thomas Lewis were trading with Lisbon and Brittany, and William Colston was apparently swindled in Bordeaux by a London shipowner. André Simon says that the Bordeaux trade recovered some of its importance during the reign of Henry VIII and that "occasionally a wine-laden ship was brought to Chepstow, but there does not appear to have existed a regular import trade at that place."

In the 14th and 15th centuries, ships returning from Bordeaux and La Rochelle would put into Bourgneuf Bay to collect salt, which by the middle of the 15th century was possibly a quarter of the value of the wine imports. Ships voyaging to Spain could load salt at Lisbon, Oporto, or Cadiz, and by the 16th century more salt came from the Peninsula than from France. The importance of salt in early times cannot be exaggerated. In 1469 the Earl of Pembroke made arrangements for his burial at Tintern Abbey and bequeathed a hundred tons of salt which he had at Chepstow to build his tomb and "the remainder of the same to build the new cloisters there."

In 1534 we find a record of the payment of 22d. for the carriage of 22 casks of wine from Le Bake to Chepstow castle and Simon tells us that in 1538 "a Portuguese ship was captured and brought to Chepstow, where her cargo of Romeny wine was sold."

About 1550 Thomas Pope loaded 90 tuns of white wine in a Portuguese carvel and on its arrival in Chepstow re-exported the wine in smaller vessels. This practice of breaking bulk to evade customs was well known to officials, and when a cargo arrived in Bridgwater, John White, the Deputy Butler there, took two tuns on the grounds that "the King ought not to be defrauded of his prisage wines by the colour of such frauds." Thomas Pope then complained to the Court of Augmentations that "all customs and duties in the Port of Chepstow belong to the Earl of Worcester as Lord Marcher there. He and his ancestors and all others, whose estates he has in Chepstow have always had all manner of customs of wines and other wares coming from the seas by way of merchandise in that port." The Court's verdict is not known, but it is clear that Marcher rights were still being asserted.

From 1559 a system of tunnage at 3s. a tun on all wine imported was gradually substituted for previous customs and this, at least temporarily, increased Chepstow's importance for merchants wishing to avoid paying customs at Bristol. The tunnage on wine and poundage on other goods were introduced gradually because of the "long and dangerous travail" of the alien merchants. In 1562 it appeared that trade at Chepstow was unaffected: "The erle of Worcester is lorde of that porte and of the Towne and dwells in a fayer Castell and his officer geveth lycence and maketh the coquetts" (parchment receipts).

The following year "An Acte Touching Certayn Politique Constitutions made for the Maintenance of the Navye" brought in places which had previously escaped paying duty, but foreigners were allowed to import wine from La Rochelle and up to 100 tuns of other wine to Chepstow, and similarly 100 tuns to the Isle of Man and 100 tuns to Wales and Newport.

Ten years later Englishmen were still evading customs by using Chepstow for landing wine. After Andrew Vynion of Exeter and Richard Dane of Bristol had brought Gascon wine to Chepstow without paying tunnage to the Queen, a messenger was sent to investigate and, instead of receiving satisfaction and an apology, was called by the Steward of Chepstow a "false knave" and accused of troubling merchants trading with "my lord, his brother's port," where he alleged Elizabeth had no authority. The Steward threatened to put the messenger in the pillory with his ears nailed while he sent to the Earl of Worcester in London for instructions, and was very reluctant to release him. Possibly is was this incident which led to the opening of a custom house in Chepstow in 1573.

THE PORT IN TUDOR TIMES

At the time the authority of the Lords of the Marches was abolished in 1536, John Leland wrote: "To Chepstow may cum great shyppes." Most of the ships which entered the Wye at that time were in fact very small, to judge from the limited information that survives. In October, 1565 we know of *Le Trynitie de Chepstow* (12 tons, Philip Johns, master) taking 60 stone of wool from Tenby to Minehead. The only ship from Wales mentioned in Hakluyt's *Voyages* is a 10-ton vessel from Chepstow, and that was probably the usual size of a coaster.

Hakluyt's description is worth reproducing here, as it is the only account which gives us some idea of the human beings on those vessels which are now mere names and tonnages. Laurence Aldersey sailed in 1586 for Egypt and writes: "I embarked my selfe at Bristoll, in the *Hercules*, a good ship of London, and set saile the 21 day of Februarie, about ten of the clocke in the morning, having a merry winde: But the 23 day, there arose a very great storme, and in the mids of it we descried a small boat of the burden of ten tunnes, with foure men in her, in very great danger, who called a maine for our helpe. Whereupon our Master made towardes them, and tooke them into our ship, and let the boate, which was laden with timber, and appertained to Chepstow, to runne a drift. . . Thursday the 16 day of March, we had a sight of the streights, (i.e. Gibraltar) and of the coast of Barbary. The 18 day we passed them, and sailed towards Patras. Upon the 23 of March, we met with the *Centurion* of London which came from Genoa, by whom we sent letters to England, and the foure men also whom we tooke in, upon the coast of England."

This boat was mentioned because of a chance rescue, and even ships which appear in customs returns do not give more than a hint of the amount of trade, since they are simply the vessels with cargoes liable to duty which the officials bothered to enter and do not include trows and other coastal craft. Isolated in a largely unrecorded past are *Le Charitie de Chepstow* (70 tons, master John Tege) which arrived in Chepstow on January 2nd, 1580 from Bordeaux with a cargo of wine, prunes, rosin and vinegar; *Le Elizabethe de Chepstow* (30 tons, master, James Webber), which brought iron and train oil from San Sebastian on June 13th; and *The Francis of Horsepyll* (23 tons, master, William Davies) which, on December 27th, 1586, arrived with "400 pieces Raisons in frayles and 20 poncheons raisions."

The iron and train oil may have been for the wire-works at Tintern, which was beginning to bring trade to the Wye. Elizabeth I and her ministers were anxious to become independent of Continental manufacturers and to start a brass industry in England. In 1565, William Humphry, the Assay Master at the Mint, had to report that Hans Loner, the best German brass manufacturer, had refused to bring the art into this country, but hinted that he had carried out some industrial espionage: "Already fearing casualty of death in this man I have secretly prepared such Englishmen as shall more suddenly learn than he expecteth." A company was formed called the Governors, Assistants, and Society of Minerals and Battery Works, and Humphry and

Christopher Schutz were authorised to search for calamine or ore of zinc which was necessary to mix with copper to make brass. In June Humphry and Schutz found calamine near Bristol, but the rivers were all sluggish or working mills, so the two men crossed the Severn and selected the Angidy brook at Tintern for the site of their works. Brass was first made at Tintern in 1568, but it was the wireworks there which became more successful, mainly because of a demand for carding wool. Chepstow ships took the wire to Gloucester, Bristol, and London. By 1587 the works employed about 150 people and was making a profit.

In 1573 there were customs houses at Chepstow, Cardiff, and Swansea, and Chepstow became part of the official port of Cardiff. It must have been difficult for the Earl of Worcester and Chepstow merchants to resign themselves to a loss of privileges, and in fact many of the early port books are blank. In 1578 the Collector at Cardiff appointed deputies in all the creeks and pills as far east as Chepstow, but his own officers in Cardiff did not set a very good example, and David Roberts was accused of "receyving the Pyratts and theyr spoyles" and John Millom was "for sundrie fowle and notorious misdemeanours and offences against him found," sent to the pillory, imprisoned, and dismissed.

In 1585 the inhabitants of the ports of Chepstow, Newport, Cardiff, Neath, and Swansea were united in their indignation against a new impost on "such wynes as are and shalbe there discharged and spent onlie and not transported from thence by water to any porte in England where imposte was and is usually paid." They alleged that they had formerly been liable to duty only when they re-exported the wine and that Elizabeth was the first monarch to force this duty upon them. "And whereas sondrie shippes of great burden have byn belonginge to the foresaid portes nowe there are fewe or non' but small barkes of xviij or xx tie tonnes."

They also complained that they had to pay the Lords Marcher "for mizes in respect of allowance of their ancient im'unities, lybertyes, and franchises, but allso do pay unto the foresaid porte certen customes and other duties due to them as lords marchers." But the old ways were gone, and by the end of Elizabeth's reign Chepstow merchants were accepting the royal customs.

SMUGGLERS AND SEA-ROBBERS

Pirates swarmed in the Bristol Channel from at least the 13th century, and smugglers were always welcomed by the isolated population along the coast. The authorities in South Wales ports were notorious for turning a blind eye to lawless activities and even for taking part in them. The steward of Chepstow, Thomas Saundres, allowed Richard Wodelok (who had been imprisoned on suspicion of piracy) to leave the port with his ship and cargo for a payment of 20s., but in this instance the lord claimed that the cargo ought to have been forfeited to him, and a Court of Great Sessions in May, 1415 fined the steward £80.

In 1440, for example, *La Marie* of Bilbao, sailing under the King's safe conduct was wrecked off Belle Isle and her cargo of iron was brought to Chepstow and disappeared without trace. In 1478 the Lundy pirate Colin Dolphin was very active, and during the reign of Henry VIII William Chick terrorised the Bristol Channel. He was described as "the chief champyon amongest them," and J. W. Dawson quotes from the Star Chamber records that when he came in the "companye of the pyratts from Bristoll to Cardiff - saieth that he cam over at the passinge of Auste and from thens he came by lande to this towne."

The pirates and smugglers were hardly less evil than their so-called betters. As an example, a ship called the *Valentine* was sold at Chepstow for £100 to Richard Abbys of London by Sir Thomas Sperte, who had already sold it to Richard Hore, also of London. Hore arrested the ship at San Lucar in Andalusia and arrived in Cogan Pill in August, 1538 with a cargo of wine, salt alum, and tunny. The Earl of Worcester's agent, Walter Herbert of Chepstow (possibly the same man who owned a ship which was captured by Breton pirates and found to contain among the cargo falcons, handguns, crossbows, and "other artillery") seized the *Valentine* for failure to pay dues and for having on board some Portuguese nationals fleeing from justice in their own country.

Richard Hore was imprisoned in Cardiff castle, but released to bring the Portuguese for examination. He brought some of them to the castle, but the rest escaped, including a woman named Agnes Fernandez who fled into the woods and died there. Hore was again arrested and at the inquest on the woman, two of the Portuguese accused him of being the cause of her death. Although "the said enquest could understond nor know what the portingals did say, but by the report of oon James, servaunt to Water herbert," the coroner committed Hore on a charge of manslaughter. He was imprisoned in Cardiff castle, but soon transferred to Chepstow.

William Herbert of Chepstow with twenty other men took the *Valentine* from Cogan Pill to Chepstow "& in that time did spend wyne and victualls, & somtymes shott the ordynauncs & so wasted artillary." At Chepstow "a certayn p'son namyng hym self baylly wt a horne aboute his necke" boarded the *Valentine* and took Richard Hore back to Cardiff. The unfortunate man remained a prisoner there until he was released by order of Thomas Cromwell. He immediately brought a case in the Court of Star Chamber against the Earl of Worcester (the Constable of Cardiff castle and Lord of Chepstow) for the tyrannous actions of Herbert and the coroner.

It was often difficult to distinguish between smuggling, piracy and privateering. The Council in the Marches of Wales was constantly investigating piracy by Moors from Algiers and the Barbary Coast, but pirates openly visited Pembroke and Cardiff, and some of the practitioners belonged to families of standing, like John Callice, the Morgans, and the Morrises.

John Callice was born at Tintern, left home at the age of 11, and was brought up by a London alderman, who sent the boy on trading voyages overseas. In 1573 Callice failed to return to

London, but turned up instead at Penarth on board a Portuguese vessel he had captured near the Azores. Callice sold his cargo of sugar and bought a ship called the *Olyphant* in which he raided merchant ships with great profit to himself. Even when he was blown as far west as Newfoundland he seized the opportunity to rob the French fishing fleet of their catch of cod.

At this time there was little difference between the pirates and the privateers who operated from the Huguenot port of La Rochelle under the flag of the Prince de Condé or William of Orange against the ships of Catholic France. John Callice entered the Huguenot service for a time and sailed with letters of marque.

In May, 1575 a 240-ton vessel called *The Castle of Comfort* serving under licence from La Rochelle captured *Le Sauveur* of Catholic St. Malo, landed the crew in Ireland, and brought the ship as a prize to Chepstow. The owner of *Le Sauveur* claimed that the privateer belonged to Sir Richard Grenville and William Hawkins and that they had employed a French captain named Jolliffe to hide the real ownership. Grenville and Hawkins maintained that they had sold the ship to Captain Jolliffe who "being first assaulted and shot at by the articulate ship called *The Saviour*, and after a number of *The Castle of Comfort* were hurt and one slain, did prevail against the said ship, and boarded and apprehended the same." A. L. Rowse, after examining the evidence, came to the conclusion that the St. Malo merchant was not compensated for his loss. Pirates from St. Malo often entered the Bristol Channel at this period.

Between 1575 and 1577 John Callice entered into partnership with the notorious pirate Robert Hicks and terrified all honest merchants. One day he attacked a Danish ship with a cargo of raisons, almonds, olives, and wines, which had anchored off the Sussex coast. He killed some of the crew and took the provisions which had been on their way to Copenhagen for the King and Danish aristocracy. Greater efforts were made to capture him, and shortly afterwards he was caught by the Governor of the Isle of Wight and sent to the Tower of London. Instead of being hanged he was pardoned by the Queen, took up piracy again, and was killed off the coast of Barbary about 1587.

Elizabeth was not very successful in putting down piracy, and did not set a good example by her own actions. James I and Charles I fared even worse. In 1613-4 four ships-of-war were fitted out at Bristol to protect trade, but the pirates simply went away and reappeared like flies as soon as the ships had gone. Lundy was held by a pirate called Salkeld who called himself King of the island. In August 1625 three Turkish pirates captured Lundy and threatened to burn Ilfracombe, and in 1636 four Turkish ships captured twenty vessels in the Bristol Channel. In 1626, when Charles I demanded from the port of Cardiff, which included Chepstow, a 30-ton barque with crew and provisions, he was informed that only five ships belonging to the port reached that standard and they had all been captured by pirates of Sallee.

THE 17th CENTURY

After the loss of its Marcher privileges Chepstow's trade declined and became mainly coastal, but some local ships went as far as Bordeaux and Portugal. On December 29th, 1606 the *Jennet of Austroder* brought Gascon wine to Chepstow, as did the *Ffawkon of Minsterworth* on November 26th 1607, and other ships sailed to the Peninsula for Bristol merchants. The wine trade would probably have improved if it had not been for the King's practice of rewarding favoured individuals by granting them monopolies. One of those so privileged was the Earl of Worcester who, on September 11th, 1607 was granted "all wines and doles of wine called 'pryse' wines" and all butlerage in Chepstow, Swansea, and Gower.

The earl now became as staunch a champion of the royal rights as his ancestors had been to oppose them. His agent, Charles Somerset, alleged plots to defraud the crown by bringing quantities of wine and dividing them "into several ladings and bottoms under the number of ten tunnes in each." One example of this practice of "breaking bulk" to avoid payment of prise occurred when the merchants James Pepper and Thomas Bearne brought 28 tuns of French wine in the *Mary Grace* for Bristol, but landed some of it in Milford Haven, where they claimed they were driven by bad weather.

By the same grant of James I, the Earl of Worcester also had the right to take cargoes from ships wrecked in the Severn within the bounds of the old marcher lordship of Chepstow. The earl must have profited considerably from this deplorable privilege, but we know only of instances when records were taken in courts of law, as when the earl claimed that a band of men went on board the wreck of a Dutch or Flemish ship, broke open chests of gold and silver, and took not only valuables but also cheeses, a rapier, 2lbs. of "indico," "Brasell wood," and some vinegar; to which the reply was that the ship had been wrecked within the limits and liberties of the city of Bristol and had only been driven into the earl's bounds by the current.

In the early part of the 17th century there was no such thing as surplus tonnage, and a ship usually did not leave port until it had found a cargo. In 1632 the average size of a coaster was 15.7 tons and three years later there was only one ship of over 200 tons anywhere in Wales.

John Byrd was Collector of Customs for the Port of Cardiff for most of the period from 1635 to 1662. He received a salary of £30 a year and a further £10 as Comptroller. He lived in Caerleon, then a place of greater trade than Newport, but went to Cardiff when he "heard of the arrival of any shipping." His deputies in the sub-ports were very badly paid and until 1648 charged fees to shipowners and merchants. But by 1701 customs officers at Chepstow were receiving annual salaries amounting to £105.

In 1641 customs receipts at Chepstow were returned as nil. There was a good deal of smuggling along the coast, including "Barbathoes tobaccoe" and "pruens." During the Civil War, Sir William Waller seized Chepstow castle and found a valuable ship in the river called *The Dragon.* Two years later, while Charles I was in Monmouthshire, a large ship ran aground at Chepstow and was seized for the Raglan garrison. Later, a Bristol ship of 55 tons, the *Jonathan,* arrived in Chepstow and tobacco was taken from it by order of the governor. The Civil War and Commonwealth was an unhappy time for Chepstow. There was no wine trade, though coastwise exports of timber continued. In

From Samuel and Nathaniel Buck's View of Chepstow, 1732

Red Rocks by S. Ireland, 1797. Modern Bulwark was built on the high land in the background. At the right is the Rock House Inn, and the Rock Shipyard lay between this and the Portwall
(By Courtesy of Chepstow Museum)

The Wye near the old timber yards by F. Dayes, about 1800
(By Courtesy of Chepstow Museum)

Warehouses and shipping at Chepstow about 1840 by J. H. Robinson and G. Childs
(By Courtesy of S. F. Aitken, Esq.)

Chepstow from Tutshill by George Hillier, 1846, showing the dry dock, the "Wye" steamer, and warehouses (including the tall building below the church which became the bobbin factory and later the "Bob Inn").

The Guy Wharf between Chepstow bridge and the castle, by J. Newman, about 1850

Gunstock Wharf and George Fryer's shipyard.
The ship on the stocks is probably the "Clara," launched in 1873

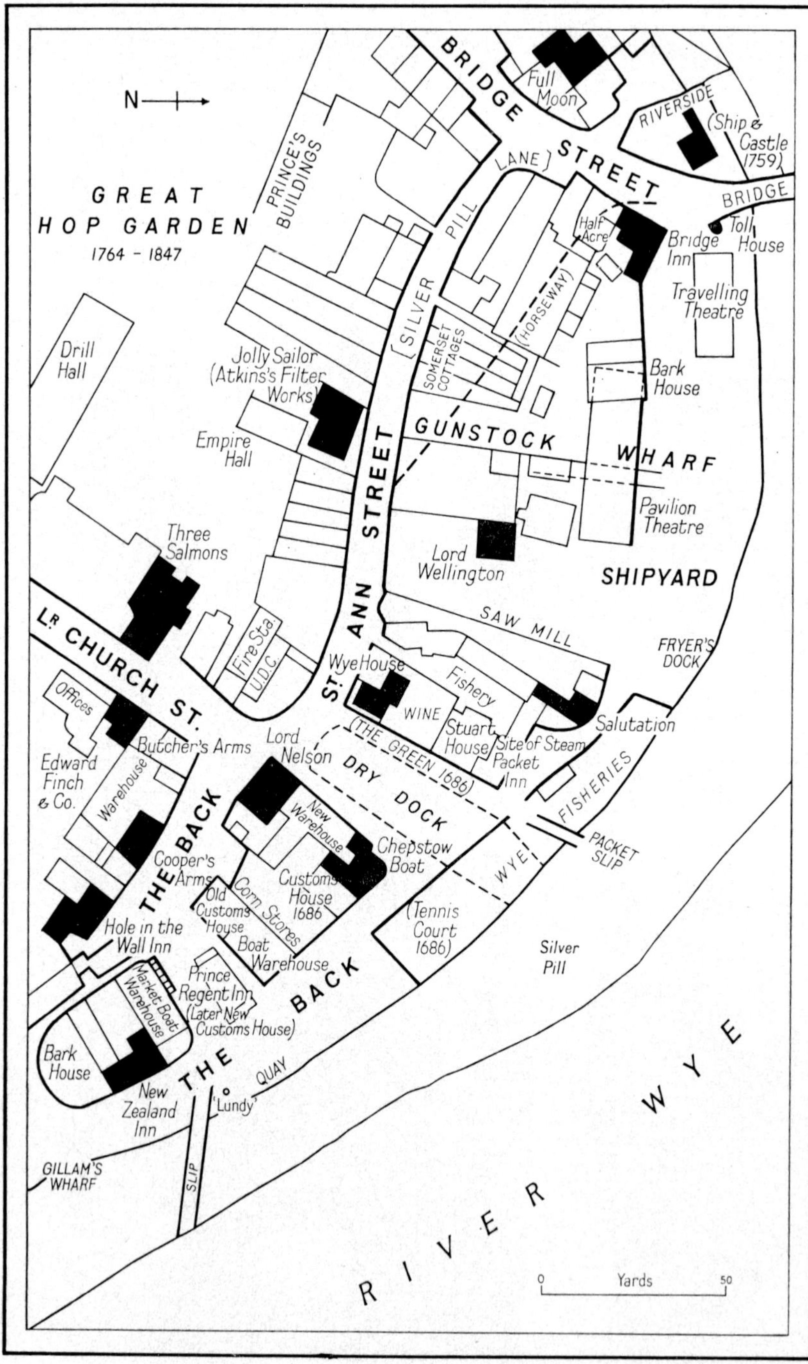

Map of part of the old port of Chepstow by Bryan Woodfield

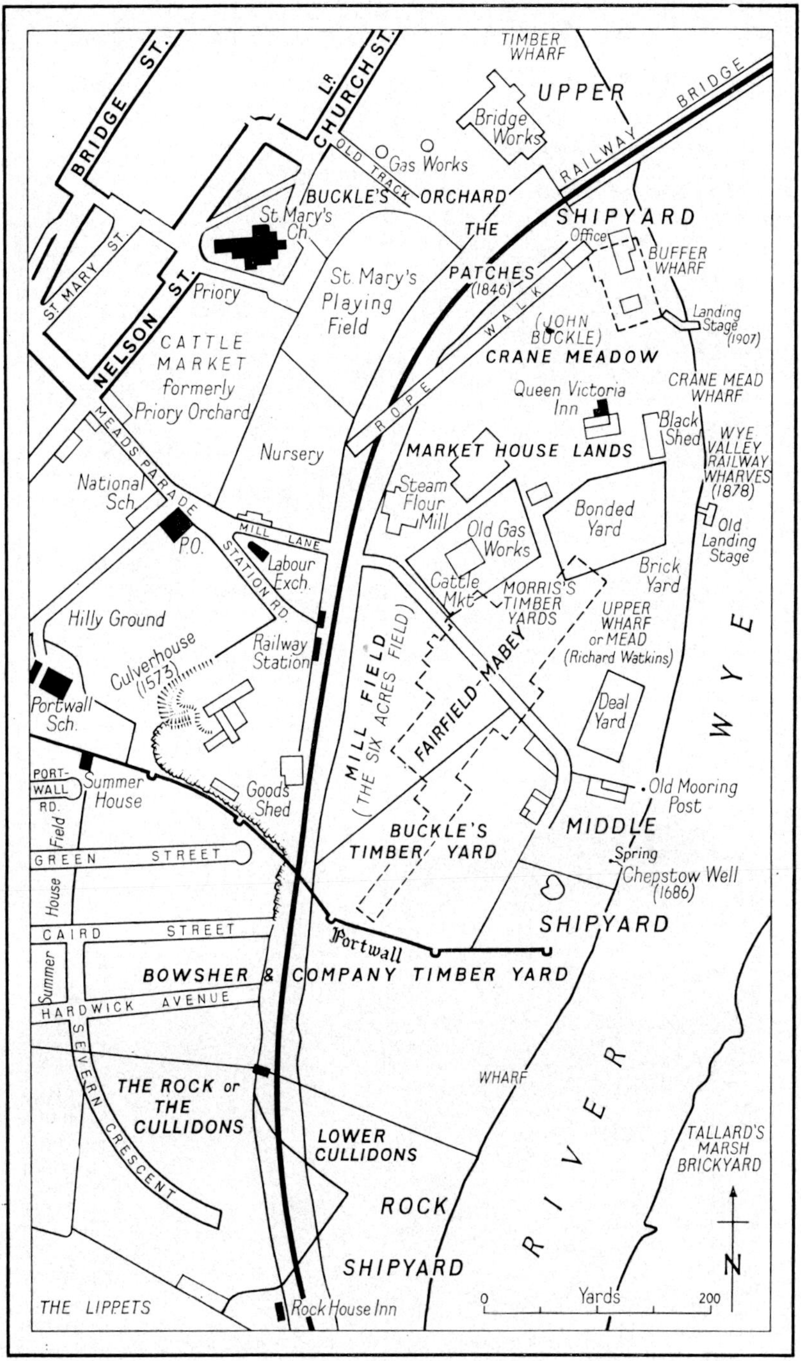

Map of the timberyards and shipyards by Bryan Woodfield

An old view of Tintern with typical river craft

Old bark houses at Chepstow about 1952

Site of the dry dock with old wine stores and fishery buildings

A trow in full sail
(By Courtesy of S. F. Aitken, Esq.)

The steamship "Rougemont", 1525 tons, the first large vessel built at Chepstow by Edward Finch & Co., 1882. *(By Courtesy of Chepstow Museum)*

The "Alice" at the Bridge Coal Wharf about 1900

Giles Sims's trow "Palace" at Lancaut about 1930

Women workers at National Shipyard No. 1, Chepstow in 1918

Ships on the stocks at National Shipyard No. 1, Chepstow in 1918
(By Courtesy of Chepstow Museum)

The Wye Fishery slip at Chepstow, formerly the packet slip.

Buffer Wharf

1656 Chepstow lost its status as a borough. After the Restoration a new custom house was built and in 1671 the Crown resumed direct administration of the customs. According to W. H. James the custom house had "a baronial fire place and handsome stairs and was graced with the king's arms bearing the date 1670."

Most of the trade was probably from the Tintern iron and wire works. By the end of Elizabeth's reign over 600 workers were employed in Tintern and wire was exported to France, Turkey, and the Barbary States. The wire was not necessarily carried in Chepstow ships, but some of it may have been. Specific information is lacking, but we find the wealthy Chepstow widow Margaret Cleyton (whose first husband Thomas Shipman and other relations had been prominent merchants in the port) mentioning in her will made on January 20th, 1626/7, among numerous other items, "my best girdle wh my cosin Lawrence Madocke sent me from Morocko." Coastal trade is well documented, and we know that large quantities of iron went to Newport, Gloucester, Bridgewater, and Bristol. Tintern also exported some cast iron goods such as firebacks, most of them marketed through Samuel Wallis of Bristol.

There must have been a fairly considerable trade after the Restoration, for 50 men were taken by the press-gangs at Chepstow in 1671-2 for the Third Dutch War. In 1682 Chepstow exported 1,372 tons of iron, the bulk of it to Bristol and Newport, but some to Gloucester, Carmarthen, and other places. Vessels were not large, and the average shipment was 16.7 tons. Most of the Tintern wire was sent to Samuel Wallis in Bristol, but there were also agencies in London, Gloucester, and Bewdley.

About 1690 copperworks, probably managed by Swedes, were started at Redbrook and ore and smelted copper became part of Chepstow's trade. The works were probably started because of the proximity of copper ore, but the Forest mines were exhausted before the end of the century. In 1690 Chepstow imported 50 tons of copper ore from St. Ives, and this quantity had grown to an annual tonnage of about 1,000 tons by 1697. Smelted copper was first exported from Chepstow in 1693, and thereafter about 60 tons left the port every year, most of it to Gloucester. The copper industry was considered to be of such importance that seamen bringing ore from St. Ives, Truro, Plymouth, and Fowey were protected from being impressed into the Navy. Copper smelting at Redbrook ceased in 1790 and was replaced by the manufacture of tinplate.

There was no difficulty in taking small barges to Redbrook on the tide, but the possibility of using the upper Wye for commerce had always been frustrated by landowners who wished to use the river for mills or fisheries. During the 17th century a number of acts of Parliament tried to make the river navigable by destroying the weirs. In 1697 the Duke of Beaufort and the Marquis of Worcester received £2,700 in compensation for the removal of weirs, but retained the fishing rights. It became possible to trade as far as Monmouth in boats with a shallow draught, and after a further Act in 1727 barges could even reach Hereford and Leominster. Daniel Defoe said Chepstow was "a place of very good trade" and called it "the sea port for all the towns seated on the Wye and Lug."

BRISTOL AND THE WYE

There was a regular market boat from Chepstow to Bristol in the 17th century, as well as a casual trade carried on in the typical Severn and Wye trows or undecked sloops. We find on August 1st, 1680 Ana Bedloe (the wife of William Bedloe, the "Popish Plot" informer) writing to her husband that she was ill in Bristol and that "Your Mother and Sister went this morning for Wales, by the Chepstow Boat." The master of the Chepstow Boat in 1726 was a leading townsman named John Gosling. This regular trader took corn, timber, wool, cider, and country produce and brought back shop goods of all kinds. Passengers usually went by way of the ferry at Beachley.

According to Defoe, Bristol merchants loaded corn at Chepstow in 1724-6 for shipment to Portugal and elsewhere, but it is difficult to determine the extent of this trade. It certainly fluctuated, and some years none at all left the Wye. From the middle of the 18th century considerable quantities were shipped to Bristol, but

David Williams, writing at a time when thousands of tons of corn were being brought down the Wye, wrote that it was not a surplus product, "For the little farmers sell immediately after harvest, to discharge their rents; and buy at advanced prices in the winter, in markets not wholly supplied by the county."

During the first thirty or forty years of the 19th century Bristol received a large part of its grain from Chepstow, which in turn received it from places farther up the Wye.

During the last decade of the 18th century, two market boats, the 70-tons *Chepstow* and the *Friends,* went to Bristol once a week and returned the following day. The *Chepstow* Boat's rival was the *Ann and Peggy* on May 15th, 1815, when the owners of the sloop *Chepstow* agreed to pay the owners of the *Ann and Peggy* £60 a year for 14 years for them to give up their trade with Bristol. In the 1790's "regular trader trows" were advertised in Bristol to sail to Chepstow, Tintern, Llandogo, Monmouth, and Hereford. Probably this was an optimistic forecast rather than a rigid time-table. The trows usually transferred cargoes and passengers at Brockweir or Llandogo into flat-bottomed barges. The best account we have of these is Charles Heath's of 1804: "Small craft sail from Monmouth to Bristol every fortnight, called the SPRING, viz. at the full and change of the moon, that city receiving large supplies of corn among other articles from this county. Goods are charged in proportion to bulk and weight, but grain is charged at 1s. 6d. per bag; allowing 24 bags of barley to the score, to make it equal in weight to the wheat."

He gave the cost of labour on the river as :

Hereford to Chepstow, with delivery of cargo and returning, per man	£1. 8s.
Hereford to Brockweir	£1. 1s.
Monmouth to Brockweir	4s. 6d.
Returning from Brockweir to Monmouth unladen	2s. 6d.
From Brockweir to Bristol with the trows	18s. 0d.

He noted that five men could return with a barge to Monmouth unladen, "but it requires the proportion of 15 men to 25 tons to haul it up when laden." In passing the weirs they fall with all their force flat on the ground "which is done by the shout of *yo, ho!* in which position they continue for a short space, when on another shout being given, they rise up, and securing their step, fall down a second time, and so on, till they gain a more peaceful and greater depth of water."

Brockweir had a considerable trade with Bristol because it was the limit to which the trows could go, and therefore cargoes and passengers from places higher up the Wye were transferred from the shallow draught barges. All the little river-ports sent oak bark down to Chepstow, and Bristol was supplied with cider from Hereford, corn from Monmouth, hoops from Llandogo, poles from Bigsweir, and faggots from Brockweir. Charles Heath explains that the Hudnalls wood "from being open to a number of families, does not arrive at any growth to render it of much value. The poor who cut it, and to whom the right belongs, make it up in small faggots, and send them by water to Bristol, where it is purchased by the bakers, to heat their ovens, who give about three-halfpence a-piece for them delivered on the quay."

TIMBER AND OAK BARK

Although the local oak forests were of great importance from the time of the Conquest, probably very little timber left the district. Some of it was used for building and much of it was turned into charcoal for the Wye Valley ironworks. The oak bark was used in local tanneries and there are no records of exports until the 18th century. The monks of Tintern had a tannery before 1241, when they were allowed to buy bark from Wentwood for twopence a load. A tannery in Chepstow is mentioned in a document of 1573 and leatherworkers appear in parish registers from 1597.

Dr J.H. Andrews has pointed out that "exports of oak bark for the Irish tanning industry appeared suddenly and almost simultaneously at many ports in England and Wales, but Chepstow soon took the lead." Exports increased from nothing in 1713 to over 700 tons in 1718. Most of the bark went to Dublin, but some to Wexford, Waterford, and Belfast. The bark was collected at Monmouth, Llandogo, Brockweir, and Tintern and brought by barge to Chepstow. There bark carriers wearing on their heads "a cross between a life buoy and a horse-collar" carried the bark into large stone warehouses to await export. The parish registers mention a number of people engaged in the trade, including cleaners (mainly women who removed the moss and lichen), choppers, and strippers. The earliest reference is to the burial on June 26th, 1635 of "Richard, a bark stripper," who was apparently a stranger and seasonal worker.

In 1781 John Byng saw on the quay "immense pipes of bark for exportation to Ireland." In 1796 the total bark exports reached the large amount of 5,199 tons, 19 cwt. The number of bark merchants rose considerably from about 1770 to a peak in the first decade of the 19th century and then declined steadily until the port closed in 1882. But in 1854 Chepstow still regulated the price of oak bark in all ports of the United Kingdom.

An advertisement in the *Gloucester Journal* for December 14th, 1725 seems to indicate that timber was being imported rather than exported at that time. "The *Kent* Snow, *Henry Darling*, Commander, lately arrived from London with Deals and empty Casks, Burthen 90 tons, four Guns, Men answerable, now riding at Anchor in the River *Wye, Chepstow*, takes in Cyder, or any other goods, for *London;* and will (if God permit) depart in a very short time. The Master may be spoke with next week at *Mr. Forde's* at the *Red-streak Tree*, or at the *Ship and Castle* in *Hereford*. N. B. Any Person may be further informed by Mr. *Robert Punter in Gloucester* where they may be supplied with several sorts of Deals, Baulks and Yew-firs at Reasonable Rates."

The great growth in Chepstow's timber trade occured towards the end of the 18th century, and particularly during the Napoleonic Wars. Some of the timber was used in the Chepstow shipyards, but much more was sent to Portsmouth, Plymouth, Deptford, and Woolwich. Archdeacon Coxe wrote that "a thousand loads per month have been occasionally shipped for the dock yards." James Clark, writing in 1827, claimed that the Chepstow firm of Bowsher, Hodges, and Watkins "supplied the government with one half of the timber used in building ships for the navy" during the Napoleonic Wars. John Bowsher, James Hodges, and Richard Watkins owned or had shares in nearly a hundred ships during the years when Chepstow's prosperity was at its height and the timber yards occupied most of the river bank between the bridge and Hardwick Cliffs.

The lumberjacks of the Wye Valley conveyed the timber on sledges, limbers, and wains to the river, which carried it in the form of rafts to the sawpits at the Meads. One method of transport is described in the account of an accident at Chepstow bridge as late as May 19th, 1863, when a small barge was apparently tugging a larger one to which between 25 and 30 tons of oak timber had been lashed to form a raft.

As the local forests became denuded, more and more timber was brought from the Baltic countries. Coxe's table of imports shows that small quantities of deals, staves, battens, and fir timber came from Russia and elsewhere during the years 1791 - 7, but in 1825 more than £11,000 was paid in duty on foreign timber imported into Chepstow. Merchants at this time included George and John Buckle, who were also shipbuilders, wine merchants, maltsters, ropemakers, and coopers; Warren Jane and numerous relations; John Kirby, for a time the partner of Richard Watkins; and the Chapman family. Oliver Chapman (1777 - 1857) captained one of his own ships to the Baltic, and his timberyard continued at Gunstock Wharf until after 1882. On June 5th, 1829, while he was master of the *Snow Emma*, Oliver Chapman saved the crew of the Norwegian brig *Familien* of Christiansand and was awarded a goblet by the King of Sweden and Norway. John Chapman was master of the *Venture* trading to St. Petersburg the same year, and numerous members of the Chapman family continued to be not only merchants but also master mariners.

In 1830 Chepstow was approved as a bonding port for timber, and a yard enclosed by a high stone wall was built at a cost of £500 and opened on May 20th. Pine timber was imported from Canada and there were re-exports of this and such items as Memel pipestaves to Bristol and Gloucester. In 1832 Newport was also approved as a bonding port for timber and Chepstow, with no coal and without its former local supplies of timber, could not compete. By 1844 wine had become a more valuable import than timber, and by 1856 the bonded yard was empty. Some trade continued for another 30 years, particularly for the Bobbin Factory in Church Street, but the great days of the timber trade were gone for ever.

WINE

By James I's grant of September 11th, 1607 the Earl of Worcester was to "have without hindrance all wines also butlerage" in Chepstow, Swansea, and Gower. Some monarchs did their best to hinder the Gascon wine trade, but the descendants of the Earl of Worcester were just as content if their prisage came from Portugal. William III discriminated by means of customs in favour of Peninsular wines so that by 1699 few English people were left in Bordeaux. Queen Anne tried to ruin the French wine trade altogether by imposing a duty of £55 a tun on French wine and only £7 a tun on Portuguese. Naturally Port wine became more popular, though the number of ships visiting Chepstow was never large. In 1753 prisage was paid on 1242 pipes, 19 butts, 114 hogsheads, and 14 quarter casks, or about 165,000 gallons.

The arrival of a ship was considered worthy of mention in the *Gloucester Journal*, for example: July 7th, 1755, "Arrived at Chepstow, the *Venus*, Capt. William Bloom, from Portugal, with Wines," or, in July, 1771, "On Monday last arrived at Chepstow, the *Elizabeth*, Capt. Wm. Butson, in 12 days from Oporto, laden with wine for Mr. Fydell." This was the Richard Fydell of whom Edward Davies wrote in 1786:

> Empty Dick's pipes, and drink his cellar dry,
> While he, well pleas'd, imports a fresh supply.
> Dick never pray'd for rain, but for sunshine,
> To ripen grapes, and fill his vats with wine.

Fydell's Almshouse Cellar was afterwards occupied by Edmund Townsend, who, on January 1st 1791 took Thomas Brown as his managing clerk at £80 per annum plus 5% of the profits. Townsend left in 1828 and Brown joined in a partnership at the Back with John Jones, who died in 1847.

In 1789 George Buckle, the Rev. Francis Lewis, and William Mutlow became wine importers at Raglan Lodge with a capital of £20,000. Partners changed from time to time, and included John Griffiths, Richard Morris, James Dowle, and Stephen Sandford. In 1839 Dowle and Sandford had "four spacious and airy vaults" at the Priory capable of holding 500 pipes and 100 hogsheads of wines and spirits. They had in bond at the beginning of the year 9,783 gallons of Portugal wine, 8,496 gallons of Spanish white wine, 387 gallons of Pontac, 342 gallons of Bronti, 1,710 gallons of Brandy, and 2,240 gallons of Rum, as well as whiskey and gin not under bond.

Bowsher, Hodges, and Watkins became importers of wines and spirits on August 27th, 1791 with a capital of £5,000 each from Bowsher and Hodges and £3,000 from Watkins. It was agreed that Watkins should allow his profits to accumulate to make his share £5,000 and that John Bowsher should have £300 a year above his share, "having been a long time established." Bowsher died in 1822 and Hodges in 1827, when Watkins concentrated his resources on the timber trade and shipbuilding.

In the later years of the 18th century Chepstow's trade with Portugal increased, with imports of 40,000 gallons in 1791 and 46,740 gallons in 1792. The right to butlerage was bought back from various nobles by the crown between 1803 and 1809, but the Duke of Beaufort was still receiving it in 1830 at the rate of 5s. a pipe or 2s. 6d. a hogshead, in addition to prisage.

Numerous members of the family of Davies or Davis were wine merchants in Chepstow. On June 8th, 1838, William Davies (in partnership with William Ambrose and John Gale) founded the Chepstow Wine and Spirit Company in premises at The Back near the Dry Dock. Dowle & Sandford became known as

Sandford & Co., with partners Stephen Sandford and Oliver Chapman. The *Chepstow Mercury* reported on January 23rd, 1864: "Shipping Intelligence. Arrived *Maria Manuela,* Triplett, master, from Oporto and Cadiz, with wines for Sandford & Co." After Sandford's death in 1871, the Priory cellars were sold and became a brewery, but the stock was purchased by Miller Brothers of the Wye Salmon Fisheries who re-opened the stores formerly occupied by the Chepstow Wine and Spirit Co. In 1875 they sold to T. W. Clarke and E. Lansdowne, but by this time most of the wine brought to Chepstow was being re-shipped from Bristol.

A Treasury Order of March 2nd, 1838 established Chepstow as a warehousing port for wines and spirits, and as a result duties received increased by more than £3,000 a year. In 1860 Gladstone lowered the duty on wine to 3s. a gallon and abolished the unfair discrimination against French producers. In 1868 the customs revenue at Chepstow included £4,472 from spirits and £756 from wine, the comparatively small sum received for wine reflecting Gladstone's support.

After Chepstow was made a bonded port, the Duke of Beaufort's agent still claimed prisage and butlerage, but on September 2nd, 1840 he complained to the customs officer at Chepstow that he had received nothing since 1838. The officer replied that he had been in the port for only a short time and that he understood the Duke was entitled to prisage but not butlerage. "I, however, think the Act of the 59th. Geo. 3, Ch. 52 would determine the matter, but at present I do not know where to lay my hand on it." This ignorance seems to have been diplomatic. On March 22nd, 1841 the Collector of Customs requested payment for supplying a return of wine imports. The Duke's agent consulted his solicitor, who tried direct action and applied for butlerage and prisage to the local merchants. Several attempts were made to claim these dues, the last being in 1844, and then the appeals lapsed until 1872. The Duke's agent wrote to his solicitor in September wondering whether "it would be possible to carry on the account at this distance of time down to the present period." He was anxious to know how much His Grace had lost and was curious enough to consider incurring the expense himself. Chepstow Custom House stated that the fee for a return of wines imported into Chepstow would be £25, and the Duke's agent, stating that he would probably have to pay the fee himself, dropped his inquiries for good.

THE RISE OF THE PORT OF CHEPSTOW

In 1700 Chepstow's status improved and it became an independent customs port with Newport as a creek, though it still remained part of the headport of Cardiff. In 1701 Chepstow had 28 vessels with an average tonnage of 27.6. Most of the trade was in wine, timber, and bark and a number of additional warehouses were built near the wharves. Several firms situated far from Chepstow had depots in the port. In 1793 the Coalbrookdale Company founded after the death of Abraham Darby in 1789, had a warehouse in Chepstow valued at £1,736,17.6. (its other warehouses were at Bristol, Falmouth, Liverpool, and London). Surprising in more ways than one was an advertisement which appeared in *Aris's Birmingham Gazette* for June 4th, 1781:

"Westmoreland Slate.
A Yard is opened at Chepstow by JOHN BALDWYN, where the public may (at any Time) be supplied with Westmoreland Slate on the following terms, viz. :-

Best (or London) Slate, at £2.12.6.	Per Ton
Seconds (or Country) Do., at £1.17.6	Per Ton

N. B. The above Prices are lower than Slate of the same Quality was ever rendered for at Chepstow. Deals, etc. as low as in Bristol.
May 12th, 1781."

In May, 1759 a dry dock opened "for the graving, caulking, repairing, and lengthening of vessels up to 500 tons burthen." The *London Chronicle* reported that a ship went in the day after the dock was opened, and was cleaned, caulked, and turned out in one tide. By 1832 the Board of Health considered it to be a cholera hazard, but it continued for some years to be used as a rubbish tip although washed by the tide. More and more rubbish was tipped into the dock and about the middle of the last century it was filled in and levelled.

A good deal of trade continued in iron ore from Whitehaven, Workington, and Lancashire ports. Apart from the official figures of shipping, we find occasional reminders of the human beings involved in the trade. In 1786 Chepstow had a pub called the Lancashire House, and the parish registers have entries which are usually more tragic, like "A strang lad from Lancashire drowned at the back was buried March 19 1735."

In the *Gloucester Journal* for August 21st, 1780, a letter from Dublin reported that a Workington vessel with a cargo of iron ore for Chepstow was captured on August 4th. "about six in the morning by a lugger privateer, half channel over, and the Captain kept prisoner on board. While the business was transacting the packet came in sight of them, and suspecting the matter, clapped her helm a lee, and steered a different course and luckily soon after met with the *Aurora* frigate, to whom she gave information of her suspicion. The *Aurora* instantly gave and continued in chace of the privateer, till about six in the evening, when the privateer was run on shore on the southern coast of our Bay. The captain of her, Pat. Dowling, and his officers, took to their boat, and got safe with much difficulty on shore."

On May 16th, 1781 John Byng saw on the quay at Chepstow "incredible numbers of iron water pipes (like cannon) each 9 feet long and weighing about 800 weight, which are going to France (by permission) but whether for the Paris aqueducts, or the King's water works is not known; near 21 miles of them are sent." They probably were cannon, for about 1787 John Wilkinson the ironmaster made pipes for the King of France's waterworks which were really "cannon in disguise" and shipped them from Chepstow.

Some of the iron was exported to Ireland, and in addition to carrying most of its oak bark to that country Chepstow ships took salt, hoops, glass bottles, timber, and cider.

By the end of the 18th century Chepstow had probably reached the peak of its trade. According to Coxe, "In 1792, the shipping belonging to this place amounted to 2,800 tons, and in 1799 was increased to 3,500; but upwards of 1,200 vessels annually enter and clear this port, including their repeated voyages."

G. W. Manby wrote in 1802, "Chepstow is now in a flourishing state, and has a trade to Norway, Russia, and Oporto, and its contiguity to Bristol may be one, and the chief, reason of its not having a greater share of importation."

SHIPBUILDING

There is no documentary reference to the actual building of ships at Chepstow until the 18th century, but presumably from early times they were built where timber was available. At the end of the 18th century and up to about the middle of the 19th there were three shipyards at Chepstow, known as Upper, Middle, and Rock. The ships were generally small, but some were built up to 600 tons. The growth of shipbuilding is reflected in the increase in imports of materials from Norway and Russia, particularly hemp, flax, pitch, tar, cables, handspikes, cordage, sailcloth, and oars.

Shipbuilders included the firms of Buckle & Davis; Bowsher, Hodges, and Watkins; Jones and Roberts; and Oliver Chapman. Among the larger vessels launched were the 500 ton *Agnes,* built for the African trade by Jones and Roberts in 1835 and the 450 ton barque *Edward* Foley for the Liverpool-Calcutta trade in 1830. The history of wooden shipbuilding at Chepstow has been so well told by Grahame Farr in his *Chepstow Ships* that the reader is advised to consult that excellent book for details.

Shipbuilding declined in the 1840s. Oliver Chapman had to close his yard because Brunel's railway bridge passed through it, but he continued to build small vessels at Gunstock Wharf, nearer the road bridge. All the shipyards closed, then, in 1856, George Fryer launched a small sloop and after a lapse of seven years built a number of vessels at Gunstock Wharf until 1881. William Hurd continued at the same yard into the present century.

Edward Finch came to Chepstow to build the railway bridge and, after its completion, remained in the town, calling his yard the Bridge Works. He built one ship, the *Alma*, 132 tons gross, in 1855. A new company called Edward Finch & Co., Ltd. was registered on May 2nd 1870 and launched a small vessel in 1879. Thereafter the firm launched several ships every year. The first large ship was the *Rougemont* of 1,525 tons gross, an iron screw steamer for John Cory & Sons of Cardiff. The yard by this time was employing nearly 500 men and boys but declined to a workforce of about 120 by the end of the century.

In 1915 Lord Inchcape and others, including the Chepstow shipbuilder J. H. Siley, started a new shipyard at the Meads, adjoining the original Finch's site, with eight slips capable of taking vessels up to 600 feet in length. In August, 1917, the Government took over the yard as National Shipyard No. 1, increased the number of slipways, and started National Shipyard No. 2 at Beachley. An unknown number of experienced shipyard workers were brought to Chepstow from the Tyne, Tees, and Clyde and about 6,000 Royal Engineers.

The first ship launched from National Shipyard No. 1 was the *War Forest* in September, 1918, but when the war ended two months later critics of nationalisation demanded the return of the yards to private ownership. The shipyard at Chepstow was bought by a sydicate called the Monmouth Shipbuilding Co., Ltd. but eventually passed to the Fairfield Shipbuilding and Engineering Co., Ltd. in 1925. During the second World War Fairfield's built three tank landing craft a month, but these were the last vessels launched at Chepstow.

THE CHEPSTOW - BRISTOL STEAM PACKET AND MARKET BOATS

Grahame Farr tells us in his "West Country Passenger Steamers" that in September 1822 the steamboat *Duke of Lancaster* was moved hurriedly from the Bristol to Cork route to forestall a rival, the *Duke of Beaufort*. The latter vessel of 58 tons was more suitable and began the run on October 7th, 1822 and continued daily until she was laid up for the winter. In 1823 the *Cambria* ran for while, but from 1824 to 1827 the *Duke of Beaufort* had a monopoly.

James Clark wrote in his Guide: "THE STEAM PACKET, *Duke of Beaufort*, for the conveyance of passengers between Bristol and Chepstow, sails daily to and fro, between the months of February and November . . . The number of visitors resorting to this town, since the establishment of the Packet, has been far greater than at any previous period . . . Fares, After cabin 4s., fore do. 3s., fore deck 2s. To and fro same day, 6s., 5s. 6d., 3s. Children under 12 half price. Refreshments of Tea, Meat, Liquors, etc. may be had on board."

Local people were as enthusiastic as the visitors about this modern miracle, and J. F. Smart published "The Steam Packet. A Poem" in 1823, wisely dedicating it to the Duke of Beaufort, who subscribed for 20 copies. In 1826 a Bristol yard launched the *Wye*, the first of three vessels so named, which was described as "a little slow snug nutshell." The second *Wye* was in service from 1843 to 1861, and the much faster third *Wye* from 1861 to 1865.

At the end of that year the owners announced that they did not intend to put her into service again, and a group of Chepstow people tried unsuccessfully to purchase her from John Jones of Bristol. The *Chepstow Weekly Advertiser* was still advertising the *Wye* steamer daily in 1871 and Kelly's directory for that year said she ran "in summer." In later years up to the outbreak of war in 1914 steam packets visited Chepstow only for excursions.

The market boats were not killed by the steam packets, but usually plied only once a week. In 1825 it was stated, "This Town, receiving most of its articles of consumption from Bristol, a large vessel, called THE CHEPSTOW BOAT under the direction of Mr. Anthony Gardiner, sen. sails regularly on Tuesdays (wind and weather permitting) and returns on Fridays." An advertisement appeared in the *Monmouthshire Merlin* on December 3rd, 1831 that Oliver Chapman's "New Chepstow Boat DISPATCH" would load at Bristol on Wednesdays and Saturdays and at Chepstow on Mondays and Thursdays and would carry corn at

4d. a sack. The advertisement drew attention to a circular announcing that the OLD Chepstow boat had reduced the cost of transport by one third or one half. "The public will not fail to discover the motives, but the NEW Chepstow Boat will ply twice a week at the same reduced rates, which are as high as they ought to be."

From about 1851 Henry Gillam was the sole proprietor of the only Chepstow Boat. The wharf near Chepstow town slip is still known as Gillam's Wharf. His was a sailing vessel which was cheaper than the steam packet, though more dependent on wind and weather. In the middle years of the century George Waters had several sloops which plied to Bristol, Newport, and Gloucester from his own coal wharf near the castle. These "Waters vessels" were not regular traders but more akin to coasters, and made longer voyages if there was a suitable cargo. Their main purpose however, was to supply the town with coal, and the last of these coal-boats, the *Alice* appears in numerous photographs up to the early years of the present century.

THE PORT IN DECLINE

Dr. J. H. Andrews has pointed out that like many small harbours situated near a major port, Chepstow had very little foreign commerce. In the 19th century foreign trade was the cause of expansion of ports, and coastal trade stagnated, yet in 1811 "no less than sixty ships, totalling 8,762 tons, left the Wye for English ports beyond Lands End, the tonnage for London exceeding that of every west-coast port (including Bristol) except Cardiff and Liverpool."

In a thriving port numerous people earned a living from the ships, from the pilot who brought the vessel through the Shoots and up the Wye to the innkeeper who quenched the seamen's thirst. Among the most important were the sail-makers, and some of the wealthier ship-owners had their own sail-lofts to make sure of a quick repair or replacement after a storm. Enormous lengths of rope were needed in a ship, so the port not only brought cables and cordage from the Baltic, but also had its own ropewalks. The largest was on the site of the present railway embankment, and there were others in Bridge Street, High Street, and St. Mary Street. Block-makers were nearly always pump-makers as well, and sometimes made masts, oars, and even figure-heads.

A large number of men earned their living from the timber trade as clerks, timber measurers, and particularly as sawyers, and a smaller number from the wine trade as coopers, hoopers, and cork-makers.

Chepstow's advantages as a port were a river navigable for many miles inland, a trade in timber, iron, and wire and its earlier fiscal privileges; but the Monmouthshire Canal made Newport much more important and of course Newport had coal and Chepstow did not. A correspondent in the *Advertiser* of March 25th, 1876 lamented that Chepstow "has been under a dark cloud since the decadence of the age of wood."

During the rejoicings for the Reform Bill in 1832 a Chepstow man observed, "For a moment I completely forgot the drooping commerce of our little town." But many merchants were still hopeful. The coastwise corn trade continued on a large scale. Chepstow became a bonding port for wines and spirits in 1838 in addition to bondings already in force for timber, hemp, linseed, tallow, tar, iron, pitch, etc. Customs receipts were £8,890 in 1844 but declined to £5,228 in 1868 .

When the railway was built in the 1850s. many local people welcomed it to revive their trade, but it had the opposite effect. J. B. Snead built an outsize bank and in due time became insolvent. Robert Sharp, a railway contractor, built a large steam flour mill, but by 1856 a gloomy correspondent to the press wrote: "I am informed that numerous vessels which arrive here with Corn &c. from abroad, for Messrs. Sharp & Co., are *compelled*, after their discharge, to proceed to one of the neighbouring ports for outward cargo. Surely if this be true, it is no wonder that trade should depart from Chepstow: that Foreign vessels should be so rarely seen in her docks."

The Wye Valley Railway Company opened a line from Chepstow to Monmouth in 1876 and again some people thought this would revive trade in the port. The company decided to build wharves extending to 800 feet and the first pile was officially driven on July 20th, 1878 amidst discharges of cannon and peals from the church bells. The first consignment was a cargo of corn from Bristol in November for the Wye Valley Mills at Redbrook. The following year the Chepstow Steam Boat Carrying Company was formed with a vessel which made two trips a week to Bristol, bringing wheat from Bristol for the steam flour mill and taking back flour.

The *Advertiser* of February 8th., 1879 asked sadly, "What of our once famous corn importation trade, under the auspices of a Jenkins, and of the now empty corn-stores on the 'Back' groaning under their heavy burthen of grain from the Baltic, the Danube, or the Black Sea?" The editor's memory must have been at fault, for the only cargo of grain his newspaper had ever reported was one brought by the brig *Arab* of Arbroath from Thessaly after voyaging out from Southampton to Balaclava in 1855.

An accurate record of the number of ships at Chepstow at midnight on April 2nd, 1871 is found in the Census Schedules, which show that there were 12 vessels in harbour, 1 at Brockweir, 2 off Beachley, and 1 in Littleton Pill. The two largest were the French brig *Jean Bart* of 177 tons and the Prince Edward Island brigantine *Princess* of 159 tons, both waiting to go up to Gloucester. More than half of the vessels were trows and barges. The trows were the last of the local ships and carried vast quantities of limestone from quarries at Lancaut and elsewhere for building the docks at Bristol, Avonmouth, Newport, Sharpness, and Gloucester.

Chepstow began as a Marcher port, and was at different times part of the headport of Bristol, Cardiff, and Gloucester. For centuries Beachley was included in the port of Bristol, but latterly had its own custom house for checking ships going up and down to Gloucester before the opening of the Sharpness Canal. Until recently both of Chepstow's custom houses survived in private occupation, the "Old" Custom House facing the square called The Back and the "New" Custom House facing the river. But in 1882 Chepstow ceased to be a customs port and by order of March 16th the same year became simply a Port Sanitary Authority.

APPENDIX

Foreign ships began to use the port of Chepstow again on Sunday, December 22nd, 1963, when the *Hendrik Holwerda,* a Dutch 500-ton motor vessel with a German crew berthed at Buffer Wharf with a cargo of Portuguese hardwood for the Sudbrook Pulp Mills. Since 1967 the firm of Medport Ltd. has controlled the shipping, much of it coastal, but some from France, Holland, Germany, and Spain. The principal imports have been timber and sand, but also fertilisers, ferro-manganese, wheat, and talc from the Shetland Islands.

THE WYE SALMON FISHERIES AND SITE OF DRY DOCK
by M. Waters

Bibliography

J. H. Andrews: "Chepstow: A Defunct Seaport of the Severn Estuary" in *Geography*.

Archaeologia Cambrensis, Vol. 65, 1911 (Q. R. Roll (Memoranda) m. 133)

Birmingham Gazette, June 4, 1781

J. A. Bradney: History of Monmouthshire, Vol. IV

A. R. Bridbury: England and the Salt Trade, Oxford, 1955

Bristol & Gloucestershire Archaeological Society Transactions, 1955

Wm. Coxe: Monmouthshire, 1801

E. M. Carus-Wilson, ed.: The Overseas Trade of Bristol in the Later Middle Ages, Vol. VII, 1937

E. M. Carus-Wilson & Olive Coleman: England's Export Trade, 1275 - 1547, Oxford, 1963

Census Schedules, 1871

James Clark: Guide, 1825, 1827

Chepstow Mercury

Chepstow Parish Registers

Chepstow Weekly Advertiser

J. W. Dawson: Commerce and Customs, Newport, 1932

Deposition Books of Bristol, Vol. I

Ifan ab Owen Edwards: Calendar of Star Chamber Proceedings, 1929

J. Goronwy Edwards: Calendar of Ancient Correspondence Concerning Wales, Cardiff, 1935

C. L'Estrange Ewen: The Golden Chalice, Paignton, 1939

Grahame E. Farr: Chepstow Ships, Chepstow, 1954 and West Country Passenger Steamers, Prescot, 1967

J. A. Fraser: Spain and the West Country, London, 1935

Gentleman's Magazine

Gloucester Journal

N. S. B. Gras: The Early English Customs System, London, 1918

Mrs J. R. Green (A. S. Green): Town Life in the 15th Century, 2 vols., London, 1894

Gwent C. R. O.: Evans & Evill MSS.; Raine 0007

Richard Hakluyt: The Principal Navigations, Voyages, etc. Glasgow, 1904, Vol. VI

Cyril Hart: Royal Forest, Oxford, 1966

Charles Heath: Tintern Abbey, 1793 and 1810; Monmouth, 1804; Chepstow, 1808.

Alfred Hillman: Historical Handbook, Chepstow, 1882

House of Commons Journals

W. T. Jackman: Development of Transportation in Modern England

W. H. James: Chepstow, 1915

Rhys Jenkins: "The Copper Works at Redbrook" in *Trans. Bristol & Glos. Arch. Soc.*, Vol. 63, 1942

B. L. C. Johnson: "New Light on the Iron Industry of the Forest of Dean" in *Trans. Bristol & Glos. Arch. Soc.*, Vol. 72, 1954

Emyr Gwynne Jones, ed.: Exchequer Proceedings (Equity) Concerning Wales, Cardiff, 1939

T. I. Jeffreys Jones: Exchequer Proceedings Concerning Wales in Tempore James I, Cardiff, 1955

W. H. Jones: History of the Port of Swansea, Carmarthen, 1922

E. A. Lewis: Welsh Port Books, London, 1927

E. A. Lewis & J. Conway Davies ed.: Records of the Court of Augmentations relating to Wales and Monmouthshire, Cardiff, 1954

E. A. Lewis: An Inventory of the Early Chancery Proceedings Concerning Wales, Cardiff, 1937

G. W. Manby: Historic and Picturesque Guide from Clifton, Bristol, 1802

John Hobson Matthews: Cardiff Records, Vol. I, Cardiff, 1898

Monmouthshire Merlin

Edward Owen, ed.: Catalogue of the Manuscripts relating to Wales in the British Museum, 1900

G. D. Owen: Elizabethan Wales, Cardiff, 1962

Eileen Power & M. M. Postan: English Trade in the Fifteenth Century, London, 1933

Proceedings and Ordinances of the Privy Council of England, Vol. IV., pp. 208 - 10

T. B. Pugh, ed.: The Marcher Lordships of South Wales, Cardiff, 1963

H. J. Randall & Wm. Rees, ed.: "Port Books for the Port of Cardiff and its Members for the Years 1606 - 1610" in *South Wales & Mon. Record Society*, III, iii, 1954

A. L. Rowse: Sir Richard Grenville, 1937

Rolls Series, Calendars

André L. Simon: History of the Wine Trade in England, 3 vols, 1906 - 9 and Wine and the Wine Trade, London, 1921

Statutes at Large

B. J. Stevens: Navigation on the Wye, Monmouth, 1955

R. H. Tawney & Eileen Power: Tudor Economic Documents, 1924

Torrington Diaries, Vol. I

D. G. Tucker: "The Stockfish Industry in Iceland" in *Industrial Archaeology*, Vol. 9, No. 2, 1972

Sir G. Warner, ed.: The Libelle of Englyshe Policye, 1436, Oxford, 1926

T. S. Willan: The English Coasting Trade, 1938, and River Navigation

David Williams: History of Monmouthshire, London, 1796

David H. Williams: The Welsh Cistercians, Pontypool, 1970

James G. Wood: The Lordship, Castle, and Town of Chepstow. 1910; Moyne's Court, 1914; Island Chapel of St. Twrog, 1922

Life of William Bedloe, 1681

Directories

Chepstow parish records now in Gwent County Record Office.

Also see by Ivor Waters:

"The Wine Trade of the Port of Chepstow", 1967;
"Leather and Oak Bark at Chepstow," 1970;
Salmon Fisheries in "Gwent Local History" No. 42, 1977.